The Way Seekers Tarot

Artwork by NDR

Written by Anna
Jedrziewski

Published by
U.S. GAMES SYSTEMS, INC.
179 Ludlow Street
Stamford, CT 06902 USA
www.usgamesinc.com

Introduction

*N*DR has brought the full force of ancient Greco-Roman patriarchical mythology to his tarot rendering and combined it with the dynamism and bold perspective of modern graphic novels. He has, however, also created these powerful illustrations through a decidedly intuitive and nurturing filter. The result is a unique deck that brings one up short over and over again as we connect with the images on the cards. The simple, pale backgrounds of The Way Seekers Tarot indicate the blank field through which the artist called to his illustrations and let them take shape. The mix-and-match of symbolism, the sometimes intense emotion in the faces, and the bold colors that elevate the traditionally-based renderings to a New Consciousness level all contribute to making The Way Seekers Tarot a deck that holds secrets that only become apparent with repeated use.

Working through the deck, I sometimes felt as if Pamela Colman Smith had tapped NDR on the shoulder and sent him the insight behind the messages she so diligently channeled through A.E. Waite's masculine perspective.

This masculine-delineated imagery, presented in an intuitive and nurturing context, highlights the balance between male and female. The mystically astute universal symbolism of the Rider-Waite-Smith deck remains intact throughout this new interpretation.

Tarot afficionados will notice that the pillars of duality appear in different guises throughout the Major Arcana. We are reminded that we always have a choice. We move forward when we are ready.

If the masculine moves forward too quickly, the feminine puts on the brakes by whatever means necessary, and vice versa. As shown in the Lovers card, the masculine polarity must acquiesce to the femine polarity in order to gain access to higher wisdom.

The cards that traditionally contain angels retain the wings attributed to those beings, sometimes indicating their elevation over the human experience, sometimes indicating that the Seeker has achieved an elevated level of perception or transcendence.

Many of you are aware of the ongoing conversation about whether or not Justice should be the eighth card and Power (Strength) the eleventh card or vice versa. I personally feel that A.E. Waite switched the cards (making Strength the eighth card and Justice the eleventh card) to create what is known in the older literature as a "blind." Blinds were created to confuse those who were seeking knowledge without doing the work to integrate the knowledge with their life experience. I understand that many will disagree with this interpretation. It is ongoing conversations such as this that have helped to keep interest in tarot alive and well for centuries.

The Major Arcana

0 ✦ The Fool

The Seeker has zeroed in on the masculine (mental) aspect, aligned it with the feminine (intuitive) aspect, reigned in the desire nature, and is heading off on an adventure that has his/her full attention. In the highest sense, the Fool is abandoning himself/herself to the fates. It is an exercise in faith. At the lower end of the vibrational scale, it is folly. Without true faith, built on a solid foundation of experience, surrender is just giving up.

Traditional Associations: Adventure. Spontaneous journey. Wonder. Trust in the universe. Misguided beliefs.

Applied Interpretation: Calculated risks. Before you decide, look at the situation all the way around the circle (360°). Consider all the potential consequences, then decide whether the possible rewards are worth the risk. Trust your instincts but don't be foolhardy.

I ✴ The Magician

The Seeker has arrived at the top of the mountain. Having passed all the required tests for this introductory level of initiation, the Seeker is now propelled back to the beginning. Looking down from the newly elevated position, the Seeker feels wonder, doubt and confusion. All the necessary tools for advancement are in place along with all the instruction needed to move forward. It is a moment of decision. Will the Seeker find the necessary strength to put experience into action and, if so, will it be for the greater good or for greed?

Traditional Associations: Will. Creativity. Manifestation. Self-confidence. Alignment.

Applied Interpretation: The completion of one level of instruction takes you to the beginning of the next level of instruction. Will you see that as opportunity or betrayal? The choices we make at these key points in our journey determine our path for lifetimes to come.

II ✦ The High Priestess

The Seeker draws in the feminine energy to illumine the masculine perceptions (knowledge). This is the beginning of true wisdom. The High Priestess looks concerned as she observes those who approach her. Do they come in truth? Are they ready? The cross on her gown appears to be the elongated cross of the descent of spirit into matter. Will those who attempt access be ready?

Traditional Associations: Gnosis. Mystery teachings. Opening to inner wisdom.

Applied Interpretation: The door to what you want will be opened if you understand how to ask for entry. It is up to you.

III ✦ The Empress

The illumined masculine has merged with the grounded feminine and all things are possible. As the vibrations are lowered to bring the luminous closer to physical reality, the Seeker must tread lightly to ensure that the will is applied for the greater good. With the ability to manifest at will comes temptation. This is the greater lesson of this card.

Traditional Associations: Fertility. Possibilities. Expansion.

Applied Interpretation: Think carefully before you set events in motion. Once unleashed, what you desire will take on a life of its own. You won't be able to easily recall what you have summoned.

IV ✦ *The Emperor*

The Seeker must make order out of all that is surveyed. It is the beginning of Sacred Geometry. Where are the boundaries? Who belongs where? If the desire nature is allowed to run wild, it will chase itself around in circles. This is the place where the Seeker learns strategy.

Traditional Associations: Law and order. Authority fueled by the feminine.

11

Patterns that create stability. Controlled sexual desire and paternity.

Applied Interpretation: Prosperity must be directed into productive channels. Unbridled passion results in chaos. The energy of creating in the material world is different from the energy of solidifying and sustaining for the long term. If you did it once, can you repeat it?

V ✦ The Hierophant

The Seeker has demonstrated the ability to turn chaos into structure, and thus society begins to turn to him/her for guidance. The Seeker wears the symbols of initiation through the three levels of body, mind and spirit. Those who seek guidance don't always understand the level at which the Seeker now functions. The journey of discovery continues and many interpret that to mean that the wisdom on offer is rudimentary. Only those who are ready to advance will recognize the elite opportunity that has been presented to them.

Traditional Associations: Dogma. Ceremony. Adherence to the accepted forms of society. Formalized religion.

Applied Interpretation: Look beyond the public ritual and find the hidden power that is within it. The secret wisdom is carried forward in plain view, but only those who have prepared themselves will see it.

VI + The Lovers

The power of opposites now looms large for the Seeker. The Masculine Polarity must acquiesce to the Feminine Polarity in order to gain access to the higher wisdom. The Archangel (often thought to be Raphael) leaves the choice to the Seeker. Will the Seeker choose enlightenment or control? This is a much more important card than most readers understand. Accepting that spiritual force can't be controlled by the will is a major lesson on the Fool's Journey.

Traditional Associations: Decisions. Seduction. Maintaining harmony between inner and outer.

Applied Interpretation: It's time to let go and trust your intuitive nature. We can never plan for every challenge. We must trust that we will be guided when we need to be.

VII + The Chariot

The Seeker arrives at an important milestone on the journey. The dual forces have been brought under control but if the Seeker lets the sense of victory pull him/her back into the desires of the Lower Self, control will be lost. If the Seeker successfully passes this test, the next level will be achieved and the journey can continue through the next seven cards.

Traditional Associations: Can be a card of greatness. Triumph. Control over the lower nature.

Applied Interpretation: Success brings new challenges. The balance between achievement and humility must be carefully maintained.

VIII + *Power*

Having gone around the Wheel repeatedly, the Seeker has finally released his/her grip on permanence in the physical world. The desire nature is free to express its full force because it now resides above the world of inspiration. The intuitive nature has learned to control the desire nature with alignment rather than force. They have become a team.

Traditional Associations: Ease of self-control. Inherent spiritual power. Choosing the higher nature over the base instincts.

Applied Interpretation: The will can now be trusted to move the desire nature into elevated realms. The decision to walk the higher path is no longer a matter of choice. It is ingrained.

IX ✦ *The Hermit*

Having chosen truth over illusion, the Seeker begins the journey up the mountain at night. Holding the lamp out in front to illuminate the way, the Seeker comes to realize that he/she is holding the lamp for those who come behind. It is then that the Seeker recognizes the Point of Light on the path that lies ahead.

Traditional Associations: Relying upon your own judgment. Caution. When the student is ready, the teacher will come.

Applied Interpretation: When you realize that you have been serving fear instead of love, you can look beyond yourself and understand that service is the only road to enlightenment.

X ✦ The Wheel of Fortune

The Seeker succeeds in making it to the top of the mountain. There is a glimpse of heaven at the top just before the last initiate on the Wheel lets go of his grip at the bottom and releases the Wheel to turn again in its natural cycle. The Seeker has gained insight and strength but is disappointed in the search for permanence.

Traditional Associations: Twist of fate, for better or worse. Knowledge of the laws of chance.

Applied Interpretation: Success at a worldly goal is fleeting. The rewards of the physical plane come and go. Only non-attachment will bring peace.

XI ✦ Justice

Having successfully brought the desire nature under control, the Seeker has earned the right to choose. Choosing to see the truth brings the consequences of awakening. Choosing denial brings another round on the wheel of illusion. When the Seeker is ready, the truth will point out the door to the next level of wisdom.

Traditional Associations: A well-balanced mind. Favorable judicial outcomes. Elimination of undesired objectives.

Applied Interpretation: The sooner we face the truth of a situation or relationship, the sooner we will be released from that challenge/lesson. Give up denial or repeat the learning experience.

XII ✦ The Hanged Man

The Seeker turns upside down, volunteering to be suspended in space. Whatever was kept hidden is now released. Survival becomes a matter of surrender rather than resistance. The inverted crown chakra, freed from self-imposed limitations, begins to radiate unhindered.

Traditional Associations: Conquering material temptations. Surrender. Transformational pause.

Applied Interpretation: Detaching from the stimuli of the five senses, the querent can now "see" with the Third Eye. Cause and effect become clearly defined.

XIII ✦ *Death*

The Seeker now realizes that choosing to serve the king or the church is irrelevant. They are two paths to the same destination. With nothing left to lose, the Seeker is now free to choose to be reborn. Freedom from possessions, whether mental, emotional or physical, moves the Seeker toward the next level.

Traditional Associations: Transformation. Destruction and renewal. Unforeseen opportunities.

Applied Interpretation: Another level of possibility comes within reach, offering a second chance at a higher level.

✶XIV ✦ *Temperance*

Raised above the realm of physical sensations, the Seeker now stands aligned with the angel (often thought to be Michael), one foot on land (conscious awareness) and one foot on water (subconscious awareness). The Seeker maintains balance by pouring the essences of conscious/sun and subconscious/moon back and forth, from cup to cup, seeking the alchemy of spirit infusing matter.

Traditional Associations: Self-control. Moderation. Successful combinations. Reunion.

Applied Interpretation: It is all in our own hands. Realization of one's true power now comes into view.

✶XV ✦ *The Devil*

As the Seeker masters the secrets to accessing the subconscious wisdom,

the shadow begins to loom large.
There is a protector functioning to
keep the conscious awareness out of the
subconscious. At the mystical level,
the shadow becomes the dweller on the
threshold. It will take the Seeker back
to the beginning, if he/she is not strong
enough to endure the next round.

Traditional Associations: Self-imposed
challenges. Depression. Clinging to the
material in spite of the wisdom of the
higher path.

Applied Interpretation: Having come
this far, it would be better to pause if there
is self-doubt, rather than attempting to
achieve a goal without conviction.

XVI ✦ The Tower

As the Seeker finally summons the courage
to confront the shadow, the full power of
the Divine Feminine energy is released.
The Seeker has now accepted complete
responsibility for the choices being made.

There is no going back. The light of truth will always shine upon the circumstances at hand. If the will of the Higher Self is betrayed, it will be at great cost.

Traditional Associations: Abrupt change. Selfish ambition destroyed. Enlightenment breaks through, no matter the cost.

Applied Interpretation: The full power of the kundalini is brought into conscious awareness. Misuse it at one's peril.

XVII + The Star

The Seeker can now channel the light of the Divine at will and is capable of pouring that light into both the material world (land) and the emotional world (water). The power of the Psychic Eagle stands ready to fuel the rise of the conscious awareness when the Seeker's will requests it.

Traditional Associations: Gifts of the Spirit. Inspiration. Alignment with Divine Love.

Applied Interpretation: The connection with the Higher Self is now very strong. It becomes almost impossible to choose the lesser path.

XVIII ✦ *The Moon*

Journeying through familiar landscapes in the dark of night with only the changeable light of the lunar disk, the Seeker has now gained the ability to observe the animal natures objectively. The line between reality and imagination becomes blurred and yet the Seeker moves with surety in the uncertain light, secure in the guidance of the internalized Star. He/she hears a voice beyond the howling of desire.

Traditional Associations: Braving the unknown. Imagination. Deception. Unfoldment. Creative process.

Applied Interpretation: It is time to push through fear and trust your inner wisdom.

XIX ✦ The Sun

The innocent child is now clothed in red, the color of life in Eastern traditions. The Seeker has discovered eternal joy and understands that joy is the power that controls the spiritual sun. The Seeker has reached the level of awareness that Carl Jung called transpersonal. It is the point where the Lesser Self is absorbed into the Higher Self. All things are transcended with joy. Within true joy, nothing else exists.

Traditional Associations: Earthly happiness. Achievement. Liberation.

Applied Interpretation: When the lesser self surrenders to the greater good, all things are possible.

XX ✦ Judgment

With a clear vision of both worlds, the Seeker now calls out to those still asleep to open their eyes and arise. The goal becomes to bring as many people as possible into the spiritual light. There can be no purpose except that.

Traditional Associations: Renewal. Awakening to a higher purpose. Rebirth.

Applied Interpretation: Calling out to others to make the commitment to enlightenment. Service is the predominant responsibility. The failure to take that responsibility seriously will result in great loss from this elevated level.

XXI ✦ *The World*

Having successfully passed all the tests of the previous cards, the Seeker now experiences what A.E. Waite calls "when the morning stars sang together" and, along with those who have reached this level before him/her, shouts for joy. There is a sense of shocked awareness when the Seeker suddenly realizes how many times along the path the correct choice was blindly made, narrowly avoiding universal disaster. It will soon be time to become the Fool again and see what the next journey brings.

Traditional Associations: Change of place. Completion. Liberation. Assured success. Integration.

Applied Interpretation: Now that all that has occurred comes into focus and makes sense, it is time to make choices for the future. Will you stay or will you go?

The Minor Arcana

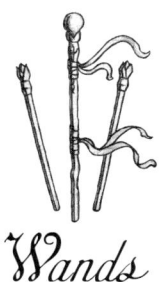

Wands

Ace of Wands

Traditional Associations: Birth. Beginnings. Invention. Source. Inheritance.

Applied Interpretation: The full power of the life force is now available. Direct your energy toward the goals of your choice.

Two of Wands

Traditional Associations: Courage and influence. Seriousness amidst grandeur. Dominion.

Applied Interpretation: Something has
been set into motion. The results are
still unclear. Maintaining the balance
between will and desire is of prime
importance at this stage.

Three of Wands

Traditional Associations: Nobility.
Realization. Established merchant.
Cooperation in business.

Applied Interpretation: Positive results
are expected but have not yet arrived.
Confidence in the enterprise will produce
what is desired.

Four of Wands

Traditional Associations: Rest.
Harmony. Healing. Romance. Harvest.

Applied Interpretation: The work has
been completed with positive results.
Celebrate the bounty to imprint the
pattern of this success in the subconscious.

Five of Wands

Traditional Associations: Battle of life. Competition. Obstacles. Lawsuits.

Applied Interpretation: Gains bring backlash. Learn to distinguish between false bravado and serious threat. Conserve energy accordingly.

Six of Wands

Traditional Associations: Victory. Success after strife. Advancement. Expectation crowned.

Applied Interpretation: Good news arrives as expected. Embrace success but remember that there is always more work to be done.

Seven of Wands

Traditional Associations: Advantage. Valor. Certain success despite opposition.

Applied Interpretation: Challengers can be held at bay. Don't surrender. Focus the will into maintaining the advantage.

Eight of Wands

Traditional Associations: Approach to a goal. Hope. Swiftness. Haste. The arrows of love.

Applied Interpretation: Maintain balance as the goal is approached. Don't relax until the end is reached.

Nine of Wands

Traditional Associations: Strength in reserve. Obstinacy. A formidable adversary.

Applied Interpretation: The boundaries have been set. Vigilance is still required but protection is at hand.

Ten of Wands

Traditional Associations: The oppression of success. Carrying a burden. Problem soon to be resolved.

Applied Interpretation: The load must be carried a little further. There are still lessons to be learned. Easy success is destructive to all involved.

Page of Wands

Traditional Associations: Family intelligence. Enthusiasm. Courage. Sudden emotion. Proclamation.

Applied Interpretation: News arrives unexpectedly with emotional impact attached. Look for the truth between the lines.

Knight of Wands

Traditional Associations: Hasty action. Change of residence. Absence. Precipitous mood.

Applied Interpretation: Quick action may be required as circumstances change unexpectedly. Be ready to respond as needed.

Queen of Wands

Traditional Associations: Love of home. Generosity, but practical in money matters. Honor.

Applied Interpretation: Emotions will fuel action on the physical plane. Be aware of the practical aspects of all decisions.

King of Wands

Traditional Associations: Agility in mind and body. Honesty. Passion. A good marriage.

Applied Interpretation: The will unites with the passion and strength required to maintain balance. Acquired skill is the active agent in maximizing this union.

Cups

Ace of Cups

Traditional Associations: Joy. Holy Table. Contentment. Great love.

Applied Interpretation: As mind, body and spirit merge, spiritual energy overflows and sends manifestation to the four directions. The doors to success are open.

Two of Cups

Traditional Associations: Union. Reciprocity. Balance between equals. Partnership.

Applied Interpretation: The opposites of the kundalini channel are intertwined and merged, giving wings to the desire nature and alignment with the one.

Three of Cups

Traditional Associations: Good fortune. Celebration. Healing at a spiritual level.

Applied Interpretation: All things are possible when the three unite in the One.

Four of Cups

Traditional Associations: Weariness. Dissatisfaction with the rewards of the material world.

Applied Interpretation: A new offer opens a way to a higher level. Don't mistake it for more of the same.

Five of Cups

Traditional Associations: Despair. Loss in love. Grieving in isolation.

Applied Interpretation: Don't get stuck in the past. Grieve the losses, but don't lose sight of what is still on offer.

Six of Cups

Traditional Associations: A gift from someone special. Memories that bring pleasure. Nostalgia.

Applied Interpretation: Help is offered from someone unexpected. Remember the good things and build on them.

Seven of Cups

Traditional Associations: Lack of focus. Illusion. Indecision. An unforeseen benefit.

Applied Interpretation: Glamour calls through despair but beware the cost of answering. A hidden source holds the answer. Look there.

Eight of Cups

Traditional Associations: A new journey begun. Disappointment in worldly success. Love abandoned.

Applied Interpretation: What previously brought joy, now brings disillusionment. Glamour has lost its hold.

Nine of Cups

Traditional Associations: Physical well-being. Earthly satisfaction. A wish granted.

Applied Interpretation: Enjoying what you have brings new riches. Mastery of the material frees the ego to move on.

Ten of Cups

Traditional Associations: True happiness. Contentment. Lasting success.

Applied Interpretation: The lessons

of the material comforts have been completed. They no longer hold power in the earthly realm. Happiness is a choice; it is not imposed externally.

Page of Cups

Traditional Associations: The birth of a child. Creativity. Imagination. News.

Applied Interpretation: Detachment from the products of the mind brings the ability to produce creatively with consistency.

Knight of Cups

Traditional Associations: Advances. A proposition. A dreamer with a purpose.

Applied Interpretation: The power of the poet brings determination in all matters. Understand your dreams before you set out in pursuit of them.

Queen of Cups

Traditional Associations: The good wife and mother. Compassion. The gift of vision. Loyalty.

Applied Interpretation: The answer is in hand but there is hesitancy to act on it. Help is delayed but not gone.

King of Cups

Traditional Associations: Accomplishments in both arts and science. Interest in religion. Generosity.

Applied Interpretation: Skill in both strategy and activity has been achieved and balanced. Good things will come from this.

Swords

Ace of Swords

Traditional Associations: Excess. Conquest. Overcoming obstacles. Triumph by force.

Applied Interpretation: Power can be grasped now. It is time to make a major move. Hesitating will cause great disruption.

Two of Swords

Traditional Associations: Stalemate. Indecision. Balance but with tension.

Applied Interpretation: It is time to turn inward and separate from external stimuli. A temporary pause won't change the situation, but it will give you a new perspective on it.

Three of Swords

Traditional Associations: Strife. Upheaval. Disruption. Heartbreak. Delay.

Applied Interpretation: This card can signal death in some form on the physical plane. Whether emotional, symbolic or material, there is real loss to be dealt with. The pain is great but so are the lessons to be learned.

Four of Swords

Traditional Associations: Rest after battle. Relaxation. Release. Exile. Banishment.

Applied Interpretation: Further effort will prove futile. Withdraw and release emotional attachments. The next step will be apparent after a period of resting.

Five of Swords

Traditional Associations: Failure or conquest over others. Dishonor. Cruelty.

Applied Interpretation: Power has been gained but by what means? Swords stolen are still swords and they will need to be dealt with. All options must be carefully considered.

Six of Swords

Traditional Associations: Safe passage after turmoil. A journey in consciousness.

Applied Interpretation: Much has been lost but the prospects ahead offer renewal. Reserve judgment until arrival.

Seven of Swords

Traditional Associations: Fragile success. Attempting to take what is not yours.

Applied Interpretation: What is won by stealth will be challenged sooner or later,

and self-doubt will always be the result
of clandestine victory.

Eight of Swords

Traditional Associations: Bondage.
Indecision. Betrayal. Temporary illness.

Applied Interpretation: The danger
has passed but the bondage remains.
Fear is the captor now. Release is a
matter of choice.

Nine of Swords

Traditional Associations: Despair.
Awakening to the nightmare.
Possible death of a loved one.

Applied Interpretation: The depths of
despair have been reached. There is no
avoiding the pain. Only inner strength
will find a way forward.

Ten of Swords

Traditional Associations: Defeat. Ruin.
Disruption. Not a card of violent death.

Applied Interpretation: Surrender finally comes to end the pain. There appears to be nothing left to salvage. Rebirth is only possible after completely letting go.

Page of Swords

Traditional Associations: Vigilance. Spying. Preparing to face the enemy.

Applied Interpretation: The news might not be good but awareness will pave the way for survival. Accept the truth and act accordingly.

Knight of Swords

Traditional Associations: Courage. Coming or going of misfortune. Skill. Opposition.

Applied Interpretation: Chivalry is not dead. Misfortune can be faced in a way that brings great gain. The depths of strength are brought to the surface.

Queen of Swords

Traditional Associations: One who has been chastened. Mourning. Privation. Personal sorrow.

Applied Interpretation: It is time to face the truth. No further progress can be made without a cold, hard look at reality.

King of Swords

Traditional Associations: Law and order. Wise counsel. Authority that has been earned.

Applied Interpretation: Situations become clear. The consequences of decisions cannot be avoided. There are tough issues that must be faced and judged appropriately.

Pentacles

Ace of Pentacles

Traditional Associations: Ecstasy. Prosperity. Contentment. The beginning of material gain.

Applied Interpretation: Mastery of the material world brings great comfort. What is sought with these skills will determine the spiritual gains that are made.

Two of Pentacles

Traditional Associations: Finding balance during change. Recreation.

Agitation. Launching a new project.

Applied Interpretation: Equilibrium is a skill that must be mastered in order to make consistent forward progress.

Three of Pentacles

Traditional Associations: Skill. Mastery. Material gain. Renown. Collaboration.

Applied Interpretation: Practice brings accomplishment. The degree of difficulty determines the degree of achievement.

Four of Pentacles

Traditional Associations: Earthly power. Inheritance. Possessions. Legacy.

Applied Interpretation: Holding on too tightly to what has been acquired blocks the flow of abundance.

Five of Pentacles

Traditional Associations: Loss. Loneliness. Dark night of the soul.

Applied Interpretation: Shared difficulties can bring mutual attraction. We are never really alone in our sorrow.

Six of Pentacles

Traditional Associations: Sharing justly. Receiving what is deserved. Vigilance in the moment.

Applied Interpretation: The gifts must be passed on. What is not shared righteously will be lost.

Seven of Pentacles

Traditional Associations: Pause in an enterprise. Success delayed or unsure.

Applied Interpretation: The seeds don't sprout right away. Anxiety must be tolerated if success is to be attained.

Eight of Pentacles

Traditional Associations: Learning a trade. Employment. Mastering a skill.

Applied Interpretation: Skill must become automatic in order to be profitable. Repeating what has been accomplished imprints it in the mind and body.

Nine of Pentacles

Traditional Associations: Material well-being. Safety. Discernment.

Applied Interpretation: Confidence within oneself brings contentment and certainty. Thoughts must not fly off on a whim.

Ten of Pentacles

Traditional Associations: Family matters. Riches. Acquiring property. Legacy.

Applied Interpretation: Union has produced progeny. Success is on display. Securing the future from here will require renewed commitment.

Page of Pentacles

Traditional Associations: Learning. New ideas. Good management.

Applied Interpretation: The acquiring of knowledge is a lengthy process and requires experience before it is of spiritual value.

Knight of Pentacles

Traditional Associations: Trustworthiness. Responsibility accepted. Patience.

Applied Interpretation: The undertaking has been accepted with an understanding of what is entailed. Perseverance will be required.

Queen of Pentacles

Traditional Associations: A noble soul. Opulence. Talents applied effectively. Earthly intelligence.

Applied Interpretation: What is needed is in hand. The future will be self-determined.

King of Pentacles

Traditional Associations: Valor. Steady temperament. Success in money matters.

Applied Interpretation: Authority in the material world requires great spiritual strength. Accumulation is not the same as ownership.

The Generator Spread

This spread is a particularly powerful companion to The Way Seekers Tarot.

Rather than a fixed answer, this spread is designed to provide information about how the energy is working around a specific situation or relationship. It then provides guidance about how the energy can be redirected to achieve the desired outcome.

Please review all the card images intently before using this deck for readings. When you feel you have connected with this deck, use whatever preparatory ritual you prefer to clear and energize the deck. Your intent and ability to focus your intellect is more important than following someone else's technique.

Spread the deck out, images up, in front of the querent and ask them to pick the card that visually seems to best represent the situation or relationship they wish to explore. You might be surprised by their choice but contain your own preconceptions and let them choose the card that they genuinely feel is best. They are providing you with valuable information. Encourage them to be truthful in their selection.

Place the card they choose in Card Position 1. Then ask the querent to shuffle and/or cut the deck to reorganize the energy around that card and what it symbolizes.

Begin taking cards off the top of the deck to build the spread's foundation. The top card will be placed in Card Position 2, the next card in Card Position 3, and the card after that one in Card Position 4. Some of you will recognize the motions of the Sign of the Cross in this placement. It is also the placement that I was taught years ago for creating a shamanic medicine wheel for ritual work. There is great power in universal symbolism.

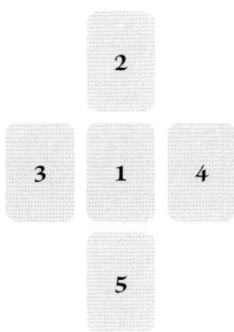

Carefully review the information that cards 2-4 provide with regard to the situation or relationship as it exists in the present moment. You might want to consider how Card 2 describes the basis of the question, how Card 3 describes contributing factors from the past, and how Card 4 describes possible outcomes in the future. Don't limit yourself to these suggestions. Let the cards tell you what they want to tell you, regardless of your preconceived ideas about the layout. Trust your instincts and your connection to the deck.

Take another look at Card 1 after you've completed the circle. Has it changed? Do you see new things in it now? The information that you are given at this stage is crucial. You must understand where the querent stands before you can give them any useful guidance.

Once you have all the information you feel you can garner from the spread as it exists, psychically ask what the querent needs to know about how the energy of the situation might be changed. Take the next card off the top of the deck and place it in Card Position 5. Look carefully at how that card's influence affects the other cards in the spread. Explore all the possibilities that the new card suggests, both alone and in connection with the previous cards.

Continue to add new cards to Card Position 5 until you feel that you have gotten as much information as possible about the situation or relationship in question. Let the querent know that he/she has choices, and suggest that the options in the spread be considered before a final choice is made.

This can be a powerful exercise. Be prepared to offer encouragement and support to the querent but be careful not to make decisions for them. The querent will choose whatever is the best route for them to use in order to progress from their present point. They may not follow the route that you would choose for yourself, but they will choose the route that is most helpful to them at the present time.

About the Artist

An experienced artist, born in one of the corners of the planet Earth, NDR has been devoted to drawing from early childhood. For many years passionate about the world of divination, he studied, practiced, and created tarot and oracle decks that have won the hearts of readers.

About the Author

Anna Jedrziewski discovered the tarot in 1970. Her first deck was *The Aquarian Tarot* by David Palladini. When she bought that deck she also purchased Eden Gray's *The Tarot Revealed*. Following Eden Gray's instructions, she began doing card readings for friends and family, using the Celtic Cross spread and relying largely on the card interpretations in the book to piece together a forecast. The resulting prognostications, sometimes negative, were alarmingly accurate. Anna stopped doing readings and began seriously studying tarot symbolism and history. The tarot captivates her to this day and she continues to learn from it.

For our complete line of tarot decks, books, meditation and yoga cards, oracle sets, and other inspirational products, please visit our website:

www.usgamesinc.com

Stay connected with us:

U.S. GAMES SYSTEMS, INC.